50 Barn Cupolas

Written and photographed
by Karl Johnson

Cupolas were first used as architectural elements during the Renaissance. Their popularity spread across Europe, and they became status symbols gracing government buildings and the homes of royalty.

Cupolas were primarily used to add aesthetic appeal to the buildings they topped. They were built in various shapes and sizes but were commonly square or octagonal. Larger cupolas sometimes had windows and were accessible by interior stairway, giving occupants a vantage point to look out over their surroundings.

Extravagant dome-shaped cupolas are often a major architectural feature on some of the world's greatest buildings.

Barn cupolas, however, evolved from functional necessity. They became an architectural feature on barns because they served a purpose.

In the late 1800s, dairy farming became a year-round commercial venture. Farmers began keeping larger herds and building bigger barns. These barns were built weather-tight to keep the cows warm and milk production high during the cold winter months. This created two new problems.

When fresh air was cut off to a dairy barn in the winter, breath from the cattle and vapor rising from cow manure stored in the barn cellar produced condensation on the floors and timbers. This could rot the wood in a few short years.

When fresh air was cut off from a barn full of hay in the summer, intense heat could build up in the hayloft to the point of spontaneous combustion.

Ventilation was necessary to prevent heat buildup and evaporate condensation.

Cupolas were mounted over a hole in the roof and often louvered to catch the wind that was forced up the sides of a slanted roof. The downward angle of the louvers kept rainwater out while allowing fresh air to flow through the cupola and down into the barn. Larger dairy barns often had two or more cupolas.

Farmers took great pride in their barns. They were the biggest single investment most farmers made. So it's understandable that many put elaborate cupolas on their barns to make a statement about their pride and prosperity. Barn cupolas were often topped with finials or weather vanes as a further statement of individuality.

The heyday of wooden barn cupolas was short. The twentieth century brought mass-produced metal ventilators that were much cheaper to produce and just as effective.

Cow manure is no longer stored under barns, hay is stored outside in large round bales wrapped in white plastic, and cows are milked in single-story milking sheds. Most old dairy barns serve little purpose other than storage, and they're very expensive to maintain.

All of the cupolas included in this book sit atop old barns. Some are well preserved or restored — some are not. Because they no longer serve a purpose, many will unfortunately fall into disrepair and be lost.

Today cupolas decorate everything from banks to motels to convenience stores; but for many of us, cupolas will always be an iconic symbol of old-time dairy farming.

Hanover, New Hampshire

Wolcott, Vermont

Newfane, Vermont

Groton, Massachusetts

Campton, New Hampshire

Sheldon, Vermont

Haverhill, New Hampshire

Greensboro, Vermont

Boscawen, New Hampshire

East Montpelier, Vermont

Harvard, Massachusetts

Lyndonville, Vermont

Concord, New Hampshire

Topsham, Vermont

Newbury, Vermont

Jericho, Vermont

New Boston, New Hampshire

Haverhill, New Hampshire

Barnet, Vermont

Bethel, Maine

Walpole, New Hampshire

Marlborough, New Hampshire

Fairfax, Vermont

Calais, Vermont

Bath, New Hampshire

Ossipee, New Hampshire

Bradford, Vermont

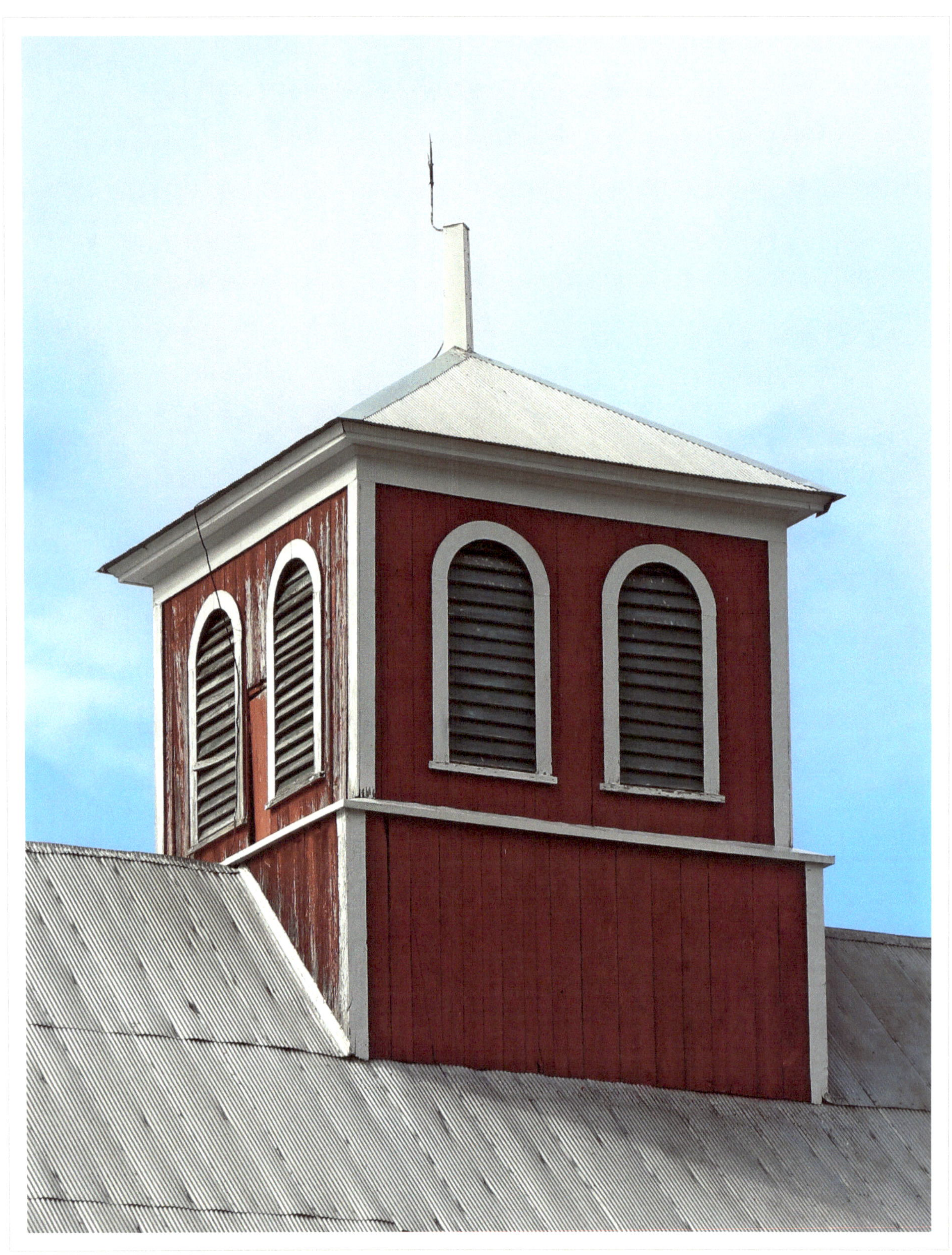

Barnet, Vermont

Bath, New Hampshire

Thetford, Vermont

Orford, New Hampshire

Waterford, Vermont

Enosburg, Vermont

Goffstown, New Hampshire

Fairlee, Vermont

Suffield, Connecticut

Hollis, New Hampshire

Cambridge, Vermont

Groton, Massachusetts

Lisbon, New Hampshire

Barnet, Vermont

Danville, Vermont

Adamant, Vermont

Hooksett, New Hampshire

Thetford, Vermont

Cambridge, Vermont

Harvard, Massachusetts

Weare, New Hampshire

Calais, Vermont

Newbury, Vermont

Hardwick, Vermont